Baptized in Moonlight

Morgan Scott

Illustrated by Dee Sanchez

ISBN: 978-0-692-03593-1

Morgan Scott

To Ben,

Thank you for always believing in my words, and for making me find myself in these poems. I am forever indebted to you for showing me what love is, and loving the parts of me that I refused to let go of, even though they make me weird. You are amazing, and I am honored to bear witness to your magic.

&

To Sawyer and Hadley,

You will always be the greatest things
that I have ever created.
Thank you for using your little hearts to make me brave.
I hope these words make you brave when you are old enough to read them.

Morgan Scott

CONTENTS

Morgan Scott

Trigger Warning

This book contains depictions of mental illness, abuse, sexual assault, disordered eating, and spiritual trauma.

If any of these topics are triggering to you, please be gentle with yourself and proceed slowly.

WANING

Waning:

1. (of the moon) having a progressively smaller part of its visible surface illuminated, so that it appears to decrease in size.

2. (v. especially of a condition or feeling) decreasing in vigor, power, or extent; becoming weaker.

We are born full.

It isn't until our environment and experiences begin to strip pieces of us away that we begin to depart from our fullest selves.

This is the story of wasting away in a world that feels too foreign and can't understand us.
The magic of childhood is shrinking and we are losing light. . .

have you seen the silent little girl
with the tangled hair?

how she swallows herself in
oversized shirts
wishing only to blend in
to her surroundings
wanting to be noticed and ignored
all at once

what if she wore her tangles
like a crown
and found the influence of
her own words?

how many poems
she could write
how many deserts she could brave
how many floods her words could cause
the strength she could discover lurking in her belly

if only someone taught her how to believe
in herself

maybe silence
is my least favorite sound
because it was my first language

but i don't live
engulfed by it anymore

and i am trying so hard
to lose the vocabulary

shadows creep
up my ceiling
and start a race
to engulf my heart
in darkness

how is it possible
to be alone
in a room full of people

and suffocating
in the company of
your fears
when you are
alone?

i was four years old the first time
i heard the words that would
follow me forever

"you talk too much"

i heard it differently -
you ask for too much
you take up too much space
you are too much
you are not enough
you are too sensitive
you believe in yourself too much

shame became
my armor
my prison
and my childhood best friend

it's desolate here
planted in this unfamiliar skin

they blame it on this empty house
but i blame it on their empty hearts

they find discomfort in my wild
and i find it unbearable to abandon
my very self in favor of their tame

i find it odd that
it's only overreacting
when i am the one
reacting

that i'm the only
one who isn't allowed
to burst out
in frustration

is it because it's only irrational
when i feel things?
or maybe because my feelings
make you aware of things
you would rather ignore

is that why i chose
to spend my life
as a gentle doormat
thanking each shoe
wearing me down
for not having spikes?

you say sensitive
as if it is a dirty word
as if you can taste the poison
dripping off your lips
when it leaves your tongue

but what you find poisonous
isn't the word at all
it is the notion that i am okay
with feeling each emotion so deeply
when all you've ever allowed yourself to feel
is anger at me for reminding you
how truly numb you are

he taught me to believe
that fists hurt in ways
that words
could not

that i should be grateful that
he didn't leave bruises
on my body
like a roadmap of his abuse

but here i am
decades later
and his words
are still breaking me

shame is our family crest
it is the switch they use to beat us down
when we get the idea that things
can be done differently

we sweep indiscretions under the rug here
because it's easier than admitting how
each generation gets more broken
than the last

my life will be dedicated
to drawing a new family crest
so that my children will never know
the fear of breaking the spell
that kept us all silent

you should never feel
forced to endure
the company of people
who commit all of their efforts
into making you feel small

don't wish them goodbye
don't wish them good luck
don't waste your wishes on them

instead
hold your wishes close
and sprint away
towards the ones who
make you feel steady

no one should be granted access
to your company
by blood alone

all i've ever wanted was to be seen
to feel worthy of being known

i was simultaneously invisible
and taking up too much space

see me for who i am
and don't tell me
my is heart wrong

because one day i will grow up
and hear your voice telling me who to be

and then you will know what it is
to be silenced
the way that i was silenced

stop acting as if
you can heal
every broken man
you meet

and first heal
the parts of yourself
that you are too afraid
to lay bare
at your feet and
to the world

stop sheltering your eyes
from the wounds
you carry like a cross

and start engaging
in the painstaking
process of growth

there is no transformation
without muscle

i struggle to grow in this dry soil
afraid the sun will scorch me
when i surface
and that the world
will devour me

i rise
a cactus
ready to bite
the first hand that
dares to touch me

i enjoy my role as
an angry plant
safe from pain
until i start to worry
that no one will stick around
to watch my flowers bloom

your purity culture
bought my silence
chained me in shame
and left me to rot
amongst the realization that
no one cared if i wasn't asking for it
so long as they could find a way to
manage the narrative

when i was broken
i became the poster child of
what not to do

i was their girl consumed by lust
and since the transaction for my silence
had already taken place
i was over-drafted and
found myself without a voice

don't throw the baby out
with the bath water
and don't throw the weekly tithe in
without the psychological mindfuck tax

this jezebel has had enough

why is it
that inspiration
refuses to strike
when you need that spark
of power
most of all?

there are moments
that i am so low
that even my art
has chosen to reject me

and without my words
do i even live anymore?

am i lost?
or do i cease to exist
at all?

art is the only thing
reminding me that
i will endure

but when the art is lost
i'm afraid that i
won't ever be able to
find myself again

i wish the world
had more people
unafraid
of being exposed

willing to be
laid bare
before the eyes
of others

wholly uncovered
in hopes of being
fully known

i seek out vulnerability
like a drug
but often i find
myself to be
the only one addicted

don't shame my tears
for falling so rapidly

because surrendering to emotion
often means facing your fears

i don't cry because i am weak
i cry because i am human

and maybe letting your tears fall
will remind you that you are too

i am so scared of being loved
because to be loved
is to let someone accept
all of the things that
made me unloveable
to everyone who came before

and how can i let him
accept those things
when i still haven't
allowed my heart
to meet my eyes
in the mirror

and tell me that i'm
deserving of my own tenderness?

sorry if i roll my eyes
as you share your
perceived expertise

maybe if your mind
was less of a boombox
and more of a window

you could actually
engage in genuine
human connection

rather than a chamber
of your own voice
echoing back to you
reminding you
how bright you are

he tells me i'm pretty
as if he has the capability
to speak it into being

and in that moment
i feel the intoxicating rush
of faked affection
and whispered crumbs
masquerading as tenderness

i inhale sharply once
surprised by his attention
i gasp again
this time shocked
at the ease
with which he crosses
every boundary i built
around my body

his hand cutting off my air
his eyes burning a hole into me
reminding me not to cry out
because no one hears the
whimpering of a ghost

and for the first time
in my short life
my ability to become invisible
has not served me well

numb feels safe now
detached and hollow
i disappear
even from my own
line of vision

free from feelings
unrestricted
in my desire to forget
that there was ever life
inside these delicate bones

numb is the place
between asleep and awake
but there is never
any rest there
for me

how broken is your heart
if you find
comfort
and intimacy
in cruelty?

do you love me?
i asked
and i had to shield my ears
because your silence was deafening

i chose to believe that love was
the absence of violence
the triumph of desirability
the comfort of familiarity

and you weren't even capable
of giving me that

just because you can
bend someone to your will
does not mean that
you should

just because she is
'too easy'
doesn't mean you
should use her up
until she is as hollow
as your heart

you aren't showcasing
your strength
by exploiting her weakness
for your own feeble arrogance

don't empty her
to try and fill yourself
because she is a sanctuary
and there is nothing in her
for someone like you

we romanticize violence
like it is our duty to swoon
at his aggression

we act as if
not taking no
for an answer
is passion
and we should
take our trembling as
a generous gift of his flattery

they say it's our fault for
not wanting to make
a home out of his anger
but who wants to live
in a house where
the walls are constantly
threatening to cave in?

tell me more
about how you punched
your friend in the face
because he degraded my body
with his words

romance me with your misogyny
as you claim me as
your property
to be degraded by
you and
you alone

all i have learned is that
the only language you speak
is violence

and that my words
will never translate
because i am
a language too foreign
for you to grasp

your words are worthy
your heart is just soft enough
you are safe here
your feelings don't make me shy away

i see you
i am proud of you
i want to sit with you in your struggle
i believe you
i accept each and every part of you

- things i wish they had said

when i buried my intentions
i wasn't holding a funeral
i was planting a garden

but you left right after the service
and you never got a chance to see me
revel in the growth of my own flowers

you chose to believe
nothing good could grow here
while i chose to make sure
that it did

your chopped up platitudes
do not quench my thirst
for soul connection

i want more than eye contact
i want our souls to reach
across the entire world
and back again
with a deeper understanding
of what it is to connect
and to be accepted

a sunset is always recognized
for its beauty

but we forget the darkness
it leaves us in
as the colors fade

maybe you are a sunset in my life
meant to be enjoyed for a short time

but leaving room for others
to be my sun, moon, and stars

NEW

New Moon:

1. (n.) the moon, either when in conjunction with the sun or soon after, being either invisible or visible only as a slender crescent.

Invisible:

1. (adj.) withdrawn from or out of sight; hidden.

Synonyms: masked, imperceptible, concealed, ghostly, buried.

This is a story of light lost.
Is it a clean slate? Or are we engulfed in darkness?
The light has turned away, and left brokenness in its place.

A reckoning has begun. . .

it is heavy
to carry my sadness
over my shoulder
every place i travel

and yet
she is the only consistent
friend that i have ever known

and there is a comfort
in knowing
that she will never
leave me

no matter how hard i try
to release her

sleep evades me
and awake leaves me
feeling empty

even babies can sleep
it is our first act as humans
after crying

and i find myself asking
why am i so good at one
and not the other?

depression is a shift in my DNA
that forces me into
an alternate existence
in which life is
no longer worth living

you can tell me
all of the life i have
to look forward to
but i can't hear you from
the other side of this glass

i can't hear anything
except the chiming
of my own self hatred
reminding me that
i don't deserve
to be here anymore

do you ever lie awake
after you have comforted
everyone else to sleep
and wonder when
it will be your turn?

your turn
to be wrapped up
in an embrace
kissed softly
and granted the gift
of sweet dreams

told just one more story
as you drift off
and finally feel free
of the responsibility
to keep everyone else
safe from harm

i purge each new bite
afraid that it will make me
somehow less worthy of love

i watch myself shrink
thinking that the smaller i am
the more worth i have

i never once stop to consider
who i am doing this for
or when i will finally
feel worthy enough
to stop

instead i choose to
keep sacrificing myself
on the altar of pretty
and hoping that
i will wake up one day
and finally be sufficient

isn't it funny
how we compliment a woman
when she is shrinking
when she is becoming smaller
and desperately trying
to take up less space?

wouldn't it be better
to ask her why she thinks
she deserves less room
than everyone else?

why her eyes look
as empty as her belly
and why her mind seems
as hungry as her body is
for something more?

a friend who only loves you
when they can control you
is not a friend at all

a person who refuses to let
your boundaries apply to them
is guilty of using you
for their own gratification

a woman who fervently degrades
other women in conversation
is doing the same to you
while you are busy
attending to her errands

wish her well
and send her on her way

your self esteem
will thank you later

you were an explosion
meant to destroy me

i missed the caution tape
distracted by your charm
because all i saw was a chance
at being adored

a chance to escape
the bombs i set off
inside of myself every night

but it turns out my shrapnel
was only meant as a departure
while your blast was inflicted
to bring complete devastation

the scariest part is
that i truly believed
that love was supposed
to feel like drowning
like abuse

so much so that
i took a nosedive into you
and never thought to consider
that i hadn't bothered to learn
how to swim

you wore a crown of daggers
that i mistook for a crown of thorns
i tricked myself into thinking
that you were my savior

because when you are drowning
a rope and a millstone look the same

i waited for you to drag me to safety
down
down
down
blissfully unaware
until my lungs filled with water
and you laughed as
i desperately tried
to propel myself upward

love is not a trap
but loving a narcissist is

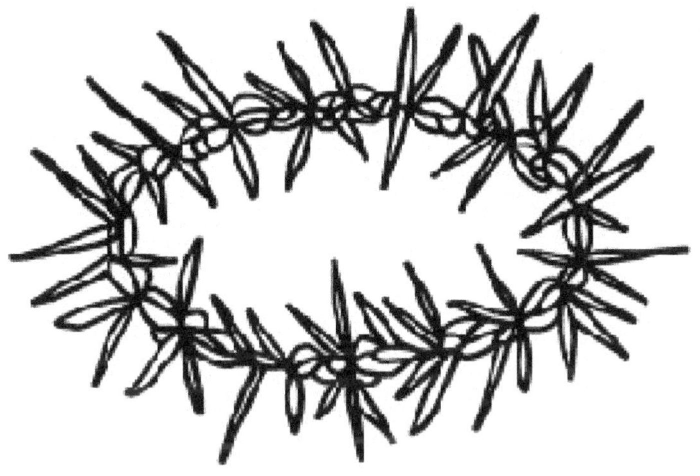

at first i worried
that you would leave
and i would miss you

then i worried
that i would leave
and you would not
miss me

and finally i worried
that i would go missing
at your hands
never to be found again

if love is a river
bending and rushing
ebbing and flowing
making a way home

then abuse is a flood
surging and choking
the life out
of everything
it comes into contact with

while somehow
maintaining the argument
that he only
drowns everything you
have ever truly loved

because he just can't
help himself

we come to an agreement
in which we both look away
when you hurt me
and pretend not to notice
as i flinch at your touch
afterwards

we both silently promise not to mention
that you never apologize
for the pain you inflict
and i pretend not to remember
the places it aches in the aftermath

we are both so
committed to our charade
that we forget that other people
can see through this deception

and it's only a matter of time
until i can see through you too

love is not slipping
not choking
it is not bending
as far backwards as your body can
until it breaks

love is not toeing the line
between anger and passion
worried that one wrong move
will land you in terror

love is not hiding yourself
trying to contort into his dream girl

love is not dumbing yourself down
to make him appear smarter

love is **not not not not not not**
the rush of air before his palm
strikes your cheek

so don't believe him when
he tells you it is
because the picture he has built of love
is one that temporarily plugs his wounds
while ripping yours open

he violates me and it
is like burning alive
i keep waiting for the sweet relief
when i succumb to the smoke
and cease to breathe

but he pulls me out of the flames
just before they consume me
as a way to remind me
that he has always held
the power
to end me
or worse

to keep me dangling
over the blaze

i torch my skin in blistering water
because i know something he doesn't

all this time he has spent setting me ablaze
has made me stronger than him
and i can withstand heat
he wouldn't dream of touching

and now
in this shower
i will burn alone
so that my dignity
may remain intact

i learned at a young age that
rage and love were easily confused
so it was easy for you to tangle me
in your thorns of romance and hate

ashamed of my body
my voice
my heart
my mind

i rejected it all and
drank the spoiled milk
you served me
and asked for an extra helping
for good measure

what was she wearing?
you ask
trying to pluck out
a reason to blame her
and not him
never him

these girls always make poor choices
you say
trying to convince yourself
it only happens to bad girls
who put themselves
into what you call
compromising situations

why didn't she fight back?
you condemn
because you don't know
how paralyzing fear can be
and how it can leave you
completely shocked and hollow

i stare out the window
silent tears rolling down my cheeks
because each time you blame her
you unknowingly blame **me too**

and i can never tell you
because i can't let you pick apart
the worst moments of my life
and tell me how if only
i had done what you would have done
i might still be whole

how much does
your silence cost?
he asked

everything
i answered

and yet he still
made me pay
with interest

you can only
punish a girl so long
for hypothetical crimes
before she becomes reckless

you can only abuse
her mind
her body
her soul
for a time
before her imprudence
becomes calculated

soon she will start
to take small pleasure
in the flickering flames
behind your eyes

because she knows
that only she can put them there
and that is enough power
to grasp on to
until she makes her clean break
and leaves you engulfed
in your own flames

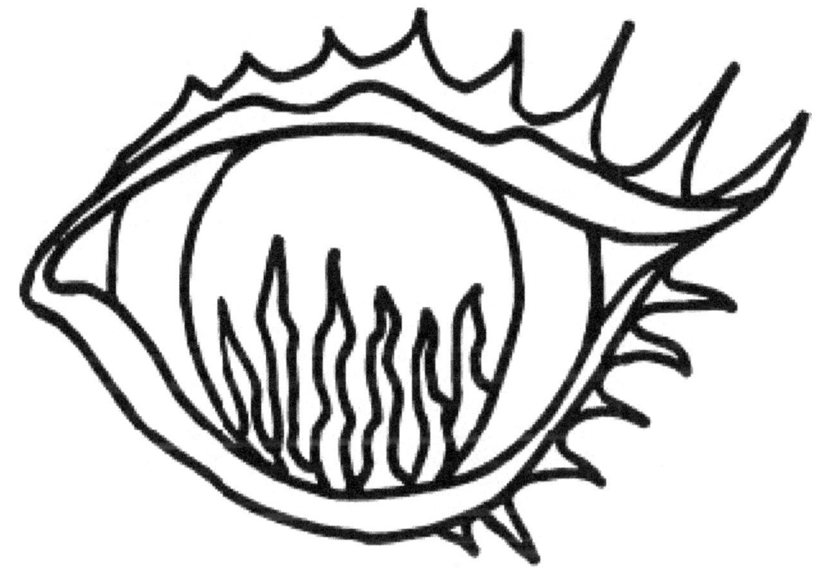

"why didn't you leave?"

because i believed that
he spoke things into being

he sucked the life out of a room
as soon as he entered it
just like he sucked the life out of me
when he entered me

he had a way of making people believe
that his power could rub off on you
if you clung to his coat
just one more time

if you stroked his skin
maybe he could transfer some of
that power to you
and heal you from all of the hurt
he had inflicted upon you

he was a lie that i believed
with every fiber of my being

my god doesn't
let people get raped
to teach them
a lesson in obedience

my god doesn't
manipulate people
into loving him

you claim to know so much
about god
but i'm starting to wonder
if you've ever met him

and why your god
and my god
seem to be reading from
completely different books

physical pain
is something you can breathe through
it has an expiration date

emotional pain
is like stabbing yourself
over and over
to make sure it still hurts

it always will
so please stop checking

emotional labor
is the price you pay
for being human

you cannot grow
while expecting
someone else to continually
spot you the cost of admission

you cannot expect them to keep
spending their last dollar
to keep you comfortable

if you were a poem
you would be full of
pretentious words
used out of context

if you were a movie
you would be a sequel
that is not half as
good as the original

if you were a meal
you would be
day old bread
and stale crackers

so stop trying to convince
me that you are anything
but leftovers and nonsense
because i am not coming back

my government says
i rape too easy
to wield any real power

my government says
a group of old men
know my needs more
than i do

my government sees me
as an incubator for their rage

i see my government
as obsolete
and will replace them
with more women who exude
quiet strength like me

these mediocre men
won't be my government
for much longer
and they will never rule me

you thought i was weak
and that i lacked the resilience
to survive anything
scary or difficult
or wicked or painful

but i survived you
didn't i?

i often find myself
wishing i could peer
into your mind

to see if you are free
of the brokenness
i have carried
since childhood

i analyze your
every move
in hopes that i can somehow
prevent myself from
asking you to carry
my suffering
on your shoulders

i'm afraid
i am afraid that you
will blame me for the
sad empty ache in the pit
of your stomach

i'm afraid that
my genes are what will
put it there

and the last thing
i want
is for you to have to
pick up sadness
worry and fear
and carry them for me. . .

. . .because you deserve
the freedom
that i so badly want
to attain

do your worst
cover me in concrete
and i will bloom
through the cracks
until i find the sun

even if i have to break
the entire earth
to get to it

i looked to the moon
to tell me who to be
but she disappeared
leaving me behind
in darkness

it's no jump in logic
to see why
after that night
i chose to try
to disappear too

WAXING

Waxing:

1. (n.) the moon at any time after new moon and before full moon, so called because its illuminated area is increasing.

Synonyms: become, build, develop, grow, increase, rise.

This is a story of resilience, of swelling and expanding. It is a story of letting go of the things that don't bring peace, and allowing ourselves to be shown compassion.

It is the start of a long journey home. . .

women are born full
full of magic
and tenderness

our hands
and our hearts
have carried the weight of
the entire galaxy
for generations

we could tap into our
mother energy
and heal the world of pain
if only you would
move out of our way

i don't need a love like sunlight
the harsh rays make me retreat into myself

i need a love like a summer drizzle
let it wash the dirt off of my soul

cool down my hot head
and baptize me in your cleansing touch

for i have been burned by sunlight
too many times

i used to believe that burning was only something
that *happened* to you
because the scars reminded me of
how powerless i felt amongst the blaze

until i realized
that when you choose to burn from within
you refine yourself in fire
burn the dead parts off and let them go
and it can't hurt you anymore

i was once broken
but i am not
made of porcelain
i am made of fire
gold and magic
and those things
can't be shattered
or destroyed

because you can
only extinguish
someone's fire
for so long
before she feels the tingling
of her own power
in her fingers
and becomes the
whole fucking forest fire
that sets your world ablaze

i hope you like burning

you can only
shove the past down
for so long before
it claws its way up
and crawls out of your mouth
as poetry

i knew i was healing
when i was finally able
to wrap my arms
around myself

and tell her that
all of the parts of her
that were too much
for everyone else

were all of the things
that made her
art to me

and that together
we could learn
to accept that art
didn't have to look like
what everyone else
thought it should

women like me
do not exist to fit
into the confined
space that you have
set aside for us
i do not live in this world
to be tolerated

sit down and watch me
exceed your wildest expectations
and don't be surprised
when i don't remember you
when all is said and done

because your perception of me
was all i had to drop to take flight

can't you see?
i absorbed the pain
and made it into art

every broken bit grew back
twice as strong
and now i am
the woman that
they warned you about

i could rewrite my story
give it less trauma
add more sparkle

but then i wouldn't be
the cathedral that i am now

a woman
built brick by brick
from the rubble
of her broken past

standing in the moonlight
firm
unmoving
unshakeable
and proud of every jagged piece
that constructed her

if someone only loves
what you do and not
who you are
it is time to release them

and in doing so
release yourself from
the vice grip
of putting everyone else first
and forgetting yourself

if i'm the one
who could never do
any better than you

why is my phone
still ringing
all these years later?

is it because you see just
how much better
i have done
now that i am
finally rid of you?

say her name
hear her story
and realize the depth to which
we are all connected

it is only when we
choose to sit with her
in her pain
that we can all collectively
begin to heal each other
and ourselves

it's the first question
hungry
dangerous men asked
when they feasted their eye
on my eighteen year old body

relationship status?

single-handedly fucking up
your patriarchal bullshit

i will no longer
hold space for the people
who demand ownership
of every corner of my mind
but refuse to hold a place for me
in their own

i will no longer let
harmful narratives
live rent free in my heart

i will give you galaxies
between us
because i can no longer
attempt to make you a home
in my life
when all you wanted
was a place to crash
when you fell on hard times

i thought my feet were made of cement
so how did you manage to sweep me off them so easily?

i thought i was made of steel
until your fingers on my skin reminded me that i was soft

i thought i was impenetrable
until i begged you to let me envelop you

i thought love was bullshit
until you kissed all of my scars
healing each one with your tenderness

you didn't flinch when i cried
as each muscle relented to your magic

you didn't run the first night
when i shook in my sleep

you didn't need me to complete you
and you didn't want to complete me

your fire didn't burn me
it kept me warm
and ignited the parts of me
that had been long snuffed out

it was always **you**

i wake up in the mess we made
and take the first deep breath
i've had in years

it fills my entire body
with a foreign substance
called hope

when i fell in love for real
i loved him because
he didn't need me
to complete him

i was so tired of
having to bend
to fit expectations

but when he looked at me
he was the first one to use
that one word to describe me -

enough

i wish you could
see what i see
whenever i catch your eye
across the room

i wish you knew how
lucky i count myself
that my hair is where you
choose to rest your fingers

i wish you knew that
you are my greatest poem
and that watching you
has inspired all of my art

they don't make them
like you anymore

and i feel inclined
to spend my entire life trying
to replicate
the magic that is you

you have
gold speckled eyes
soft tender lips
hands that hold me up
when i cannot stand on my own

and yet
you still have to
draw me out
and wait for me
to decide that
i can trust you

there is both
heartbreak and beauty
in being loved in
all of your broken places

i used to believe that
i wanted to roam
the entire world

but now i realize
i was just searching
for the peace
that i found
in your arms

i settled for everything
until i wanted you

my fear of
failure and rejection
kept me pinned
down when i wanted
so badly to fly

until someone
came along
that i wanted
badly enough
to drop all of the things
pinning me down

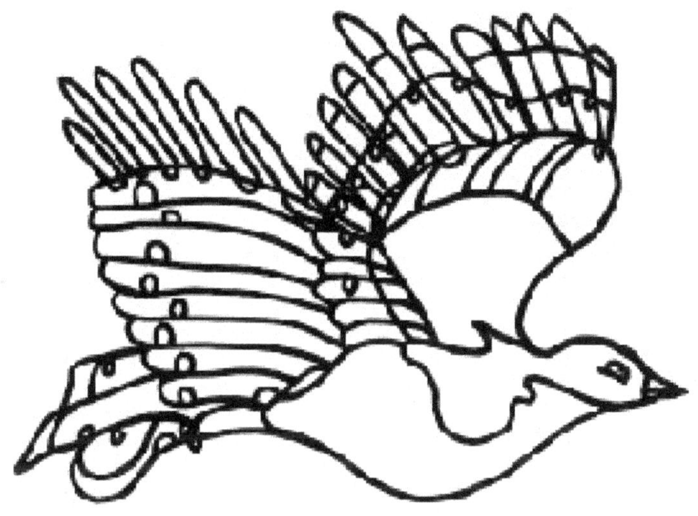

don't chase someone
who wants you
when you are the only option

don't pour yourself out
onto the floor at the feet
of people who never
savor your flavor palate

save your best
for the ones who see you
and understand
how painstaking
your journey has been

because they too
have trudged through
the carnage of loss
and the ascension
to a new peak

they nickname my chains 'freedom'
and remind me constantly to
protect my witness
refrain from being myself
in case anyone should see

they examine my brown skin
and my blue voting record
and they deem me
dangerous
a red flag

they put me on a watch list
and call it a prayer list
because i will not play
their faith games

evangelize me
with your
intentional friendships
but remember
that i will always refuse
to wear your chains
and call them jewelry

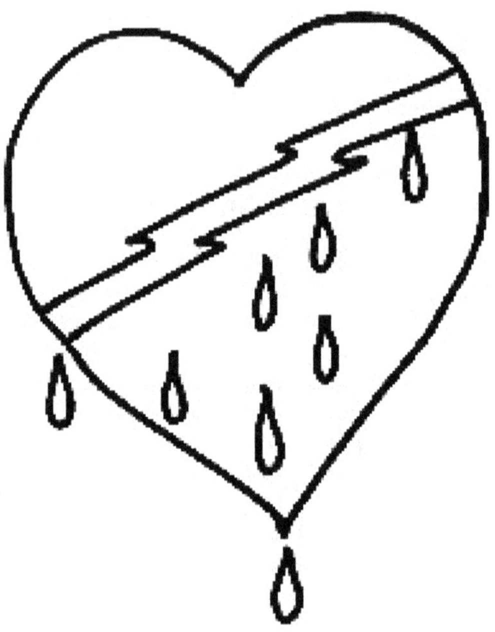

what you see as sloppy
i see as vulnerable and true

what you perceive as damaged
i know has been rebuilt
a hundred times over

what causes you to shy away
will always be the thing that
i lean into

the discomfort
of an open mind
and a bleeding heart

i wish you could free
your shackled consciousness
and see the freedom
that comes when you look
through fresh eyes

i try to make myself
smaller
quieter
devoid of curves
and flavor

to accommodate the idea
you planted in me
that my brownness
has no place in your pews

but what god
would want me to be
less than He created
for the comfort
of someone else's ignorance?

He gave me this voice
and i am going to use it
even if it makes
your ears bleed

i will empty your pews
and fill my heart
with more of His love
and less of your hostility

shame is an anchor
around my neck
dragging me down

until i recognize
the fire
within my own soul

i melt that shit and take flight

you are not just my soul mate
you are my coming home

you chase me with grace
wrap me in tenderness

you breathe life into my bones
and remind me
why i started this in the first place

nowhere ever felt like home
until i felt the chills hit
as you breathed in
all of my imperfections
and loved me still

i wish they had warned me
that while my breasts
were leaking milk and
pooling with nourishment
to sustain you

that my soul would also
be spilling out of wounds
left over from battles
fought years ago

i wish they had warned me
that love this deep can often feel
like a dull ache that never leaves
and only intensifies with each moment
that our eyes are locked
one upon the other

this chair feels like a prison
and i am a captive of time
in this waiting room

i sit
and sit
and wait
until they call my name
and i can hold you in my arms
again

finally free
to smell your scent
soak you in

and know that
you and i both
will survive this

-

motherhood is
overwhelming joy and
a constant broken heart

wishing that i could take your place
during the parts that hurt

it is the force of nature that
makes me believe that i am capable
of every single thing
the world throws at me

you make me brave

FULL

Fullness:

1. (adj.) completely filled, containing all that can be held, filled to utmost capacity

2. (n.) the moon, when the whole of its disk is illuminated, occurring when in opposition to the sun.

This is a story of redemption. It's a story of taking the thing that was empty and broken, and filling it to capacity with wonder, love, and peace.

We have been baptized in moonlight.

The light shines down and everything is illuminated and vulnerable, in the most beautiful and cleansing of moments. It is the embodiment of freedom.

Throw off the ties that bind and be welcomed home. . .

i meet her in the moonlight
and i am forced to recognize
what i had ignored for so long

she is me
before i started letting the world tell me
who i was

and for the first time
i realize how exquisite she is
and how much i have missed her
rough hands and gentle curves

we howl at the moon together
unashamed
as she sighs

welcome home
old friend

the only constant in this life
is the perpetual change
swirling around us

if only we could see
this persistent reinvention
as the gift that it is

everyday is a chance
to become someone
entirely new
and all that is asked of us
is to trust
to believe
and to bloom

i like the sea
because it reminds me
how very small
i am

and in comparison
how very big
and full of possibilities
the world is

i like to watch the waves
as they wash over my toes
and i imagine that
they could sweep me away
to somewhere completely new

honor your mind
dismiss the ramblings
of self doubt
scrub it free of judgement
and make room for
self-compassion

honor your body
soak in your own strength
and exquisite beauty
speak truth to each line and curve
and remember

you are compiled of a million
tiny specks of miracles
and you contain the keys to
heaven and hell
under your skin

your wounds
would have you believe
that your works of art
are not art at all and
that you are a copy
of someone more alluring
than you

don't ignore the wound
choose to heal it
tend to the part of yourself
that fears success
because it feels
like all of the
small failures it will take
to get there
may sink you

be tender with the wound
cleanse it
bandage it
give it time
and then let it breathe

so that now
you are free to create
all of the things you
feared would wound you further
but were really meant to heal you
body and soul

it used to bother me
when they used words like
full and supple
to describe my body

until i realized that
it doesn't matter
what they think my body looks like

because those words also describe
the life that i lead
and it is all coming full circle

people say a lady
shouldn't swear
should be quiet
should know her place

people say
a load of bullshit
to try and keep us
from being unashamed
of who we are

because shame is
the ultimate
manipulation tool
employed by the ones
who are afraid
of a world where
women don't ask
for permission
to use our influence

don't bother asking them
to be silent
instead leave them in
stunned silence
when they witness you
doing all of the things
they said you cannot

words pour out of my mouth
like a breaking dam

they gain momentum with each passing second
until they flood the entire earth

words fly out of my mind
like a swarm of bees
lead by a queen

to sting your weary soul
and to awaken you
to the parts of yourself
you had long forgotten

once i realized that i deserved
a seat at any table

i stopped trying to squeeze
in at the broken card table
with its tricks and exclusion

and made my way to the banquet hall
where i always belonged
and they had been saving my place

very rarely did God meet me
within the confines of four walls
surrounded by the perfectly timed
swelling of music
and a well rehearsed public prayer

instead he chose to meet me
in the wilderness
as i screamed into the void
and he answered back
in a whisper

He found me in the tiniest of prayers
over a sleeping baby
chubby cheeks aglow in rosy pink
lashes fluttering as she dreamed

God met me in the broken desperation
as i woke from yet another nightmare

He was there
a murmur so soft
it was almost a sigh
reminding me that His arms
would always be big enough
to wrap around all of my baggage
and still have room for me too

we are not wild like a ruckus
or even like a pack of wolves
we don't show our hand so easily

we are not wild like a roller coaster
with its predictable twists and turns
nor like a wildfire

you don't see us burn
you feel it in your belly

we are wild like rebellion
like energy
surging through your body
and out your fingertips
we are a silent riot
waiting to unleash our wild
when it is needed

we are the calm before the storm
and we are the storm itself
we are wild in secret
and now the secret is out

you say witch
like it's a bad thing
like you wouldn't
absorb my magic
if only you knew how

you are afraid of us
because you don't understand us
and the root of all fear
is ignorance and envy

maybe if you could learn to
greet the unfamiliar with
curiosity instead of distrust
we would invite you to join
our sacred sisterhood
and teach you how
to heal yourself

sisterhood means rejecting the idea
that we have to push
past one another
in order to be great

and instead
standing together
arms linked
heads high
to push past
the lies we were told

and find ourselves
reflected in one another
beautiful
strong
standing firm
in our shared power

it breaks my heart
to watch the women i love
accept emotional abuse
and call it passion

he is not passionate
he is broken
and he won't stop until
you are too

let us help each other
rise and realize
that we deserve
to wear crowns of glory
and not the bruises he leaves
on our already battered souls

there is an unspoken strength
in the ability to remain soft
in moments of extreme duress

never more exemplified
than when watching a mother
simultaneously be a ferocious lion
protecting her young

while also being the softest
place for them to rest their head
when the world tries to break them

i broke my body
as it bore them
into being

but what breaks
even more
is my heart
every time i realize
i cannot protect them
from the pain
that is living

so live, daughters
soak in every moment
and remember that
your mom
tried her hardest
to move heaven and earth
so that you could soar

and that for every tear
that falls from your eyes
i have cried a hundred more
watching you hurt

least favorite quirks of my own
have found life and magic
in their little bodies

the curve of their bellies
the softness of their souls
the loudness of their laughter
the stubbornness in their stance

i can finally see my own beauty
in the stomping of their feet
the way they bring the world
around them alight

their fire ignites my own

i didn't just give birth to them
i awoke my beauty with them
they breathed and
it was me who came to life

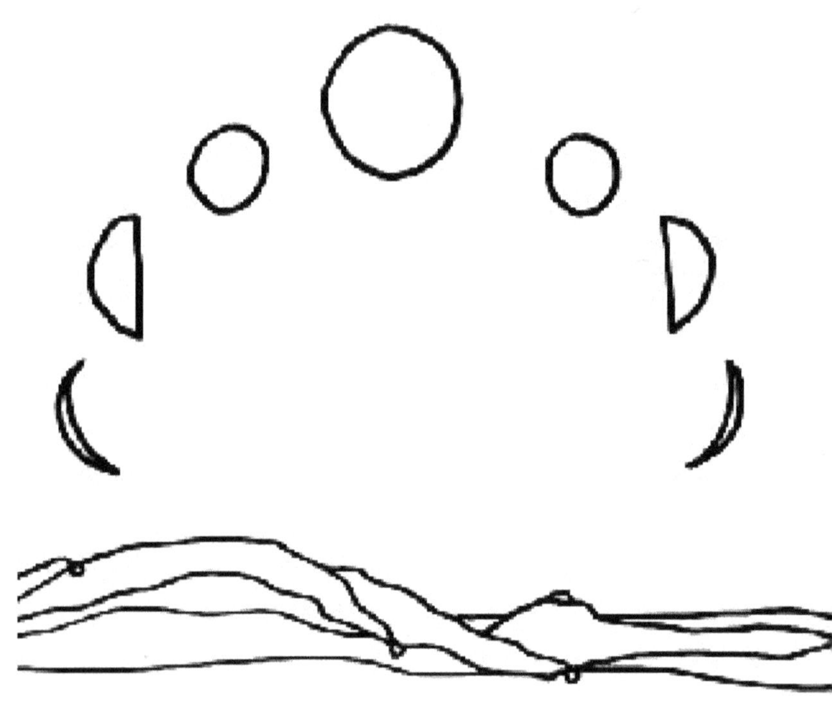

you are celestial
you engulf the entire world
with your beauty

you transform
the entirety of our surroundings
with a flick of your wrist
the oceans come crashing to life

you have the power
to awaken the sleeping
beasts in all of us
but you can also subdue us
into silence with
only your softness

and here i am
trying to remember if
you came from me
or if i came from you

you lay there
dreaming softly
not knowing
that every poem
is made up of you

you are the substance
and the softness
that makes me want
to create

you are the reason
i want a legacy
to be left
no stone left unturned
so that one day
when i am but a
whisper in the wind
you will hold my words
and say

this is the lineage of women
that i am made up of
this is who brought me
into this world

and she wrote
every single one
of these words
with me in mind

the rarest kind of love
is one that does not expect
performance

it doesn't need to feast upon
whatever you bring to the table
to find satisfaction

extraordinary love is content
to sit together
and just be

no expectations
except to be engulfed
in your presence
and to feel safe
wrapped up
in your warmth

i will not raise my daughters to be an echo
of the brokenness that built me

but rather a spark to create a new life
in which they get to be exactly who
i wasn't allowed to be

- myself, themselves

i always want to remember the way
she pushes into me with such force
as she drifts off to sleep

we become one again
even if just for a moment

she doesn't half-ass anything
not even a nap

and for once
looking at her
i experience what others see
when they admire my intensity

true love
does not wait

true love does not
wade slowly
dipping one toe
at a time

true love
deep dives
into the richness
of knowing

recognizing that it will
have to come up for air
eventually
but wishing to reside
in the depths
forever

they tell us that magic isn't real
just a fairytale we tell children
to help them
make sense of the world

they have never stopped
to feel the rain sweep them away
never believed in the magic
of a single moment
that changes everything

magic lives in the starbursts we see
when we squint our eyes
always waiting and
wanting us to believe in her

the first time
i gritted my teeth
and waited for you
to lose control

to treat my body
like a receptacle
for your wounds
and the rage
i assumed all men carried

imagine my surprise
when i got to be more than
an observer
as our souls connected
and you read the pages of my body
like they were your favorite book

i finally learned
why they titled it
making love
and i want to read this book
over and over again

heaven smiles down
on the most momentous
of occasions

because there is nothing
quite so beautiful as
the entire universe
bearing witness to
the love story of two people

as they pledge
to keep on
loving one another
through the
muck and the majesty

please don't ever forget
that you belong here
breathing in the fresh mountain air
and feeling as if you are home

you are the only one
unaware of your own magnificence
so open your eyes
wake up
and see what a treasure you are

i need you to know that
the world wants you to stay

people often ask
how i knew
you were the one

and i tell them
it is the simple truth that
at the end of each day
you are the only one
who can unwrap my heart
from her armor
and let her breathe

i trust you
with all of the raw
broken
bruised
tender
parts of my
quintessential self

and though you may fumble
as as you run your fingers over
my very soul
you never shy away
from the painful parts
of us intertwining
the fibers of our existence

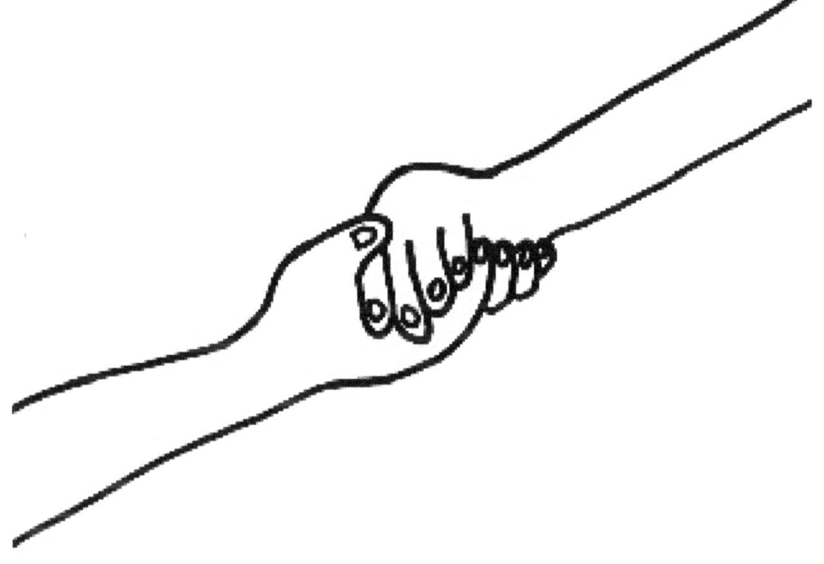

i trust the moon
even though she is
always changing

so i think
maybe it's time that
i begin to trust myself too

you dyed your
tangled mane silver
you found your voice
you learned not to
wear a mask

you embraced the things
that used to make you feel
like hiding

you elbowed your way
into adulthood
and decided not to wait
for someone to teach you how
to believe in what you could do

don’t let anyone try to
take credit for you

you did this
own it

ACKNOWLEDGEMENTS

It's hard to even know where to begin.
Thank you first and foremost to God, for using the last five years to show me that you aren't an uptight jerk like I originally was taught, and for being so incredibly creative in how you build the human mind. Thank you to my husband, Ben, for believing in me, sometimes in irrational and over-the-top ways, and for knowing I could do this way before I knew it. Thank you Sawyer and Hadley, for coloring quietly while I did all of the work to make this book a reality, and most of all for believing that your mama can do hard things. To Maggie and Pedro, for all the coffee dates where you read my words and instilled confidence in me, and for the constant reassurance that dreams are worth fighting for. You two are basically my agents and editors, and I count myself so lucky for that.
To my mom and illustrator, Dee Sanchez, for all of the babysitting, all of the creativity in my genes, and for sharing your beautiful artwork with me in this project. To my Dad, for not getting too angry at all the cuss words in this book (fingers crossed). Thank you so much to Tiffany Martinez-Durant for designing a beautiful cover to represent my work. Thank you to each and every friend who sent messages of encouragement, clinked glasses with me, commented on my poems, or told me I should write more. And thank you to each and every woman who has raised her voice to break the silence. I am here because you dared to speak up, and for that I am infinitely grateful. To my favorite poets, thank you for showing me the beauty and simplicity found in few words, and for always stirring my heart to action with your art.

And lastly, thank you, readers. If you are reading this, I can only assume you have finished this book, and that means that you have seen a part of my soul. I hope it made you feel something. I hope it encouraged you to use your own voice, and to stand up for what you believe in. Go make art.
The world needs it.

ABOUT THE AUTHOR

Morgan Scott was born and raised in Albuquerque, New Mexico and has spent most of her life having a love/hate relationship with the desert. She began writing poetry at the ripe age of eight years old, and has continued to fall in love with it her whole life. She has written for blogs, websites, and her own pleasure for many years.
This is her debut collection, but she has hopes to write books as long as she has breath. When not writing, she enjoys spending time with her husband and her two daughters, drinking chai tea, and fighting patriarchy.

Morgan can be found on

Instagram: @morgandscott
Website: morgandscott.weebly.com

ABOUT THE ILLUSTRATOR

Dee lives and works in the village of Alameda, New Mexico. She is a plein air painter and loves nothing more than taking day trips all over New Mexico and painting luscious oil paintings out of the back of her car.
She is a daily painter and wants her viewers to be transported to that place and time when she stood out in the mesas and mountains with her paints and brushes and lost herself in the wildness and beauty of the ever-changing landscape.

Dee can be found on

Instagram: @deesanchezart
Website: deesanchezpaints.com

www.ingramcontent.com/pod-product-compliance
Lightning Source LLC
Chambersburg PA
CBHW061825040426
42447CB00012B/2825

* 9 7 8 0 6 9 2 0 3 5 9 3 1 *